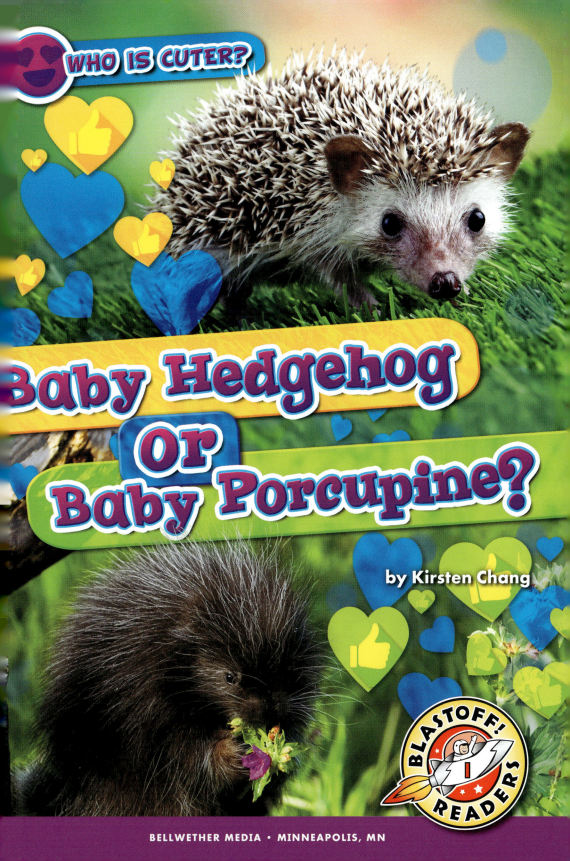

Blastoff! Readers are carefully developed by literacy experts to build reading stamina and move students toward fluency by combining standards-based content with developmentally appropriate text.

 Level 1 provides the most support through repetition of high-frequency words, light text, predictable sentence patterns, and strong visual support.

 Level 2 offers early readers a bit more challenge through varied sentences, increased text load, and text-supportive special features.

 Level 3 advances early-fluent readers toward fluency through increased text load, less reliance on photos, advancing concepts, longer sentences, and more complex special features.

★ **Blastoff! Universe**

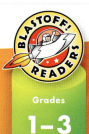

This edition first published in 2026 by Bellwether Media, Inc.

No part of this publication may be reproduced in whole or in part without written permission of the publisher. For information regarding permission, write to Bellwether Media, Inc., Attention: Permissions Department, 6012 Blue Circle Drive, Minnetonka, MN 55343.

Library of Congress Cataloging-in-Publication Data

LC record for Baby Hedgehog or Baby Porcupine? available at: https://lccn.loc.gov/2025003205

Text copyright © 2026 by Bellwether Media, Inc. BLASTOFF! READERS and associated logos are trademarks and/or registered trademarks of Bellwether Media, Inc. Bellwether Media is a division of FlutterBee Education Group.

Editor: Rachael Barnes   Designer: Brittany McIntosh

Printed in the United States of America, North Mankato, MN.

Table of Contents

Hoglets and Porcupettes	4
From Snout to Tail	8
Bugs and Plants	14
Who Is Cuter?	20
Glossary	22
To Learn More	23
Index	24

Hoglets and Porcupettes

Baby hedgehogs are called hoglets. Baby porcupines are called porcupettes.

Both babies have hard, sharp hairs. Hoglets have **spines**. Porcupettes have **quills**.

From Snout to Tail

Hoglets have small, pointed **snouts**. Porcupettes have flatter noses.

snout

Porcupettes have brown or black fur. Hoglets can be many different colors.

Hoglet tails are short. Porcupette tails are much longer!

Bugs and Plants

Hoglets curl up. Spines keep them safe. Porcupettes swing their tails. Quills keep **predators** away!

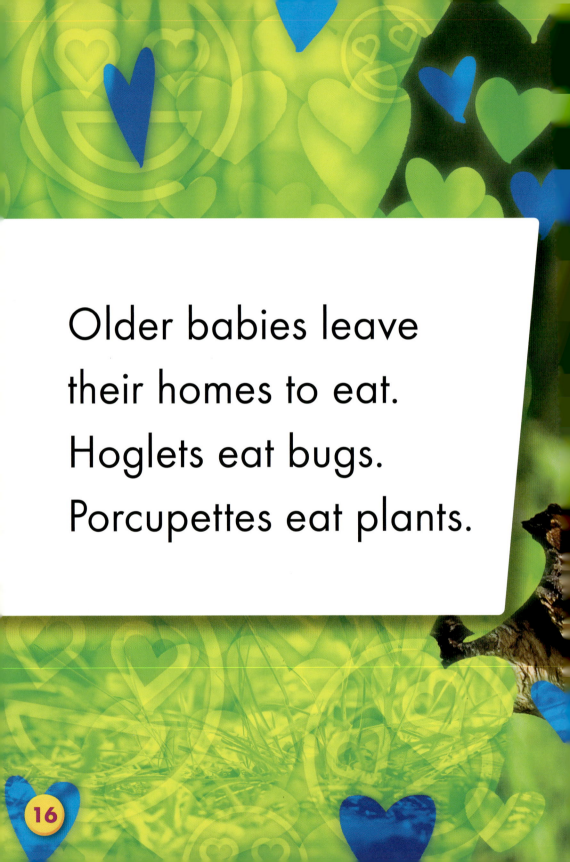

Older babies leave their homes to eat. Hoglets eat bugs. Porcupettes eat plants.

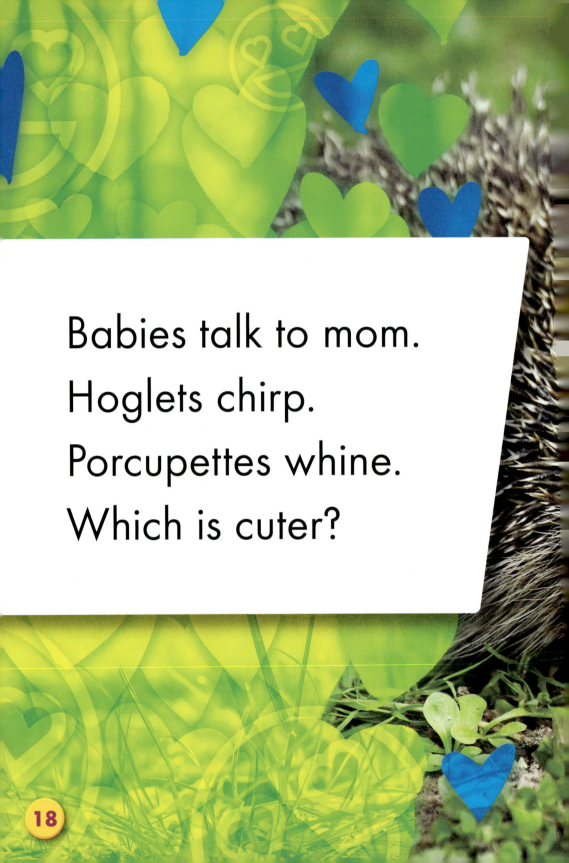

Babies talk to mom.
Hoglets chirp.
Porcupettes whine.
Which is cuter?

Who Is Cuter?

spines

short tail

pointed snout

Baby Hedgehog

curls into a ball

eats bugs

20

Glossary

predators
animals that hunt other animals for food

spines
the sharp, pointed hairs on hedgehogs

quills
the sharp, pointed hairs on porcupines

snouts
the noses and mouths of some animals

To Learn More

AT THE LIBRARY
Boothroyd, Jennifer. *Baby Porcupines.* Minneapolis, Minn.: Bearport Publishing Company, 2021.

Rice, Jamie. *Hedgehog or Porcupine?* Minneapolis, Minn.: Jump!, 2023.

Thielges, Alissa. *Curious About Hedgehogs.* Mankato, Minn.: Amicus, 2023.

ON THE WEB

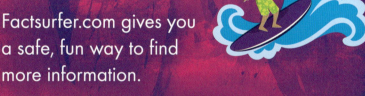

Factsurfer.com gives you a safe, fun way to find more information.

1. Go to www.factsurfer.com.
2. Enter "baby hedgehog or baby porcupine" into the search box and click 🔍.
3. Select your book cover to see a list of related content.

Index

bugs, 16
chirp, 18
colors, 10
eat, 16
fur, 10
hedgehogs, 4
mom, 18
noses, 8
plants, 16
porcupines, 4
predators, 14
quills, 6, 7, 14
snouts, 8, 9

spines, 6, 7, 14
tails, 12, 14
whine, 18

The images in this book are reproduced through the courtesy of: Kurit afshen, front cover (hedgehog); outdoorsman, front cover (porcupine), p. 21 (bottom right); brulove, p. 3 (top); Michelle Gilders/ Alamy, pp. 3 (bottom), 15 (porcupine), 21 (bottom left); Papilio/ Alamy, p. 4 (porcupine); Michiel Vaartjes/ Alamy, p. 4 (hedgehog); Geoffrey Kuchera, p. 7 (porcupine); petervallance/ Stockimo/ Alamy, p. 7 (hedgehog); Jeremy David Rhodes, p. 9 (hedgehog); M. Watsonantheo, p. 9 (porcupine); Terry Allen/ Alamy, p. 11 (porcupine); bongkarn petkhuntod, p. 11 (hedgehog); Ben Schonewille/ Alamy, p. 13 (hedgehog); robertharding/ Alamy, p. 13 (porcupine); Luca Nichetti, p. 15 (hedgehog); David Glassey/ Alamy, p. 17 (hedgehog); Design Pics Inc/ Alamy, p. 17 (porcupine); imageBROKER.com GmbH & Co. KG/ Alamy, p. 19 (porcupine); G. Lacz, p. 19 (hedgehog); Nynke van Holten, p. 20; Vladimir Bolokh, p. 20 (short tail); Viktor Sergeevich, p. 20 (bottom left); Joshua Carver/ Alamy, p. 20 (bottom right); Rosa Jay, p. 21; John Alexander Mundy, p. 22 (predators); Anan Kaewkhammul/ Alamy, p. 22 (quills); ai-ivanov, p. 22 (snouts); slowmotiongli, p. 22 (spines).